SNAIL SLIME

By Roberto Betances

 Gareth Stevens
PUBLISHING

Please visit our website, www.garethstevens.com. For a free color catalog of all our high-quality books, call toll free 1-800-542-2595 or fax 1-877-542-2596.

Library of Congress Cataloging-in-Publication Data

Betances, Roberto, author.
 Snail slime / Roberto Betances.
     pages cm. — (Nature's grossest)
 Includes bibliographical references and index.
ISBN 978-1-4824-1855-2 (pbk.)
ISBN 978-1-4824-1853-8 (6 pack)
ISBN 978-1-4824-1854-5 (library binding)
1. Snails—Juvenile literature. 2. Adaptation (Biology)—Juvenile literature. I. Title.
 QL430.4.B48 2015
 594.3—dc23

                                2014024266

Published in 2015 by
Gareth Stevens Publishing
111 East 14th Street, Suite 349
New York, NY 10003

Copyright © 2015 Gareth Stevens Publishing

Designer: Katelyn E. Reynolds
Editor: Therese Shea

Photo credits: Cover, p. 1 Jonathan Nackstrand/Shutterstock.com; pp. 3–24 (background) Oleksii Natykach/Shutterstock.com; p. 5 Will Heap/Dorling Kindersley/Getty Images; p. 7 Nailia Schwarz/Shutterstock.com; p. 9 Henrik Larsson/Shutterstock.com; p. 11 ZenShui/Odilon Dimier/PhotoAlto Agency RF Collections/Getty Images; p. 13 tijmen/Shutterstock.com; p. 15 caimacanul/Shutterstock.com; p. 17 Piotr Naskrecki/Minden Pictures/Getty Images; p. 19 yakinii/Shutterstock.com; p. 21 Scott T Slattery/Shutterstock.com.

Printed in the United States of America

CPSIA compliance information: Batch #CW15GS: For further information contact Gareth Stevens, New York, New York at 1-800-542-2595.

CONTENTS

Just One Foot. .4

Snail Species .6

Moving with Mucus 10

Staying Inside 14

Chowing Down. 18

Bubble Boat. 20

Glossary. .22

For More Information. 23

Index 24

Boldface words appear in the glossary.

Just One Foot

Could you move around on just one foot? That's what a snail does. It uses its one foot to slowly crawl. As it goes, it leaves behind a trail of slime! It's not trying to be gross. The slime helps it move.

5

Snail Species

There are thousands of kinds, or species, of snails. They can be different sizes and have shells with different shapes. All snail shells have a **spiral** on them. The shell grows and thickens as the snail gets older.

Snails have a soft body attached to their shell. They have one or two sets of **tentacles** on top of their head. Eyes that look like black dots are on the tips of one set of tentacles. However, snails can't see well.

Moving with Mucus

A snail's one foot is soft like the rest of its body. The **muscle** in the foot pushes the whole body forward. At the same time, a body part in the front of the foot **releases** a slimy **mucus**.

11

The mucus **protects** the soft snail foot from any rough **surface**. A snail can slide over a knife's edge without getting hurt! A snail's slime also helps it stick to a surface and even move upside down.

Staying Inside

Snails keep their body wet with mucus, too. They hide inside their shell on hot days so they don't dry out. Snails also hide inside their shell from predators. Many predators don't want to bite through a hard shell.

15

However, many predators eat snails, including birds, beetles, snakes, frogs, toads, and rats. When snails are scared or upset, they make bubbles with their mucus slime. The bubbles may keep some predators from getting into a snail's shell.

17

Chowing Down

Most snails eat plants, so farmers and gardeners don't like them. However, snails also munch on smaller snails, which can be helpful. Did you know that many people eat snails? You might be able to order some at a fancy restaurant!

19

Bubble Boat

Ocean snails use mucus bubbles to make boats! They float around the ocean looking for food, like jellyfish. Snail slime looks gross, but it's very handy if you're a snail! Next time you're in a garden, look around for the amazing, slow-moving snail.

GLOSSARY

mucus: a thick slime produced by the body of many animals

muscle: one of the parts of the body that allow movement

protect: to guard

release: to let something go

spiral: a shape or line that curls outward from a center point

surface: the ground

tentacle: a long, thin body part that sticks out from an animal's head or mouth

FOR MORE INFORMATION

BOOKS

Hartley, Karen, and Chris Macro. *Snail*. Chicago, IL: Heinemann Library, 2006.

Owens, L. L. *The Life Cycle of a Snail*. Mankato, MN: Child's World, 2012.

Woodward, John. *Snail*. New York, NY: Chelsea House Publishers, 2010.

WEBSITES

Giant African Snail
www.hungrypests.com/the-threat/giant-african-snail.php
See pictures of this huge snail and learn why it's a threat to crops.

Snail-World
www.snail-world.com
Read many interesting facts about these creatures.

INDEX

body 8, 10, 14

bubbles 16, 20

eyes 8

foot 4, 10, 12

head 8

mucus 10, 12, 14,
    16, 20

muscle 10

ocean snails 20

plants 18

predators 14, 16

shells 6, 8, 14, 16

species 6

spiral 6

tentacles 8